North American
INDIAN NATIONS

NATIVE PEOPLES of the SUBARCTIC

Stuart A. Kallen

LERNER PUBLICATIONS ◆ MINNEAPOLIS

The editors would like to note that we have made every effort to work with consultants from various nations, as well as fact-checkers, to ensure that the content in this series is accurate and appropriate. In addition to this title, we encourage readers to seek out content produced by the nations themselves online and in print.

Consultant: Willie Kasayulie, Chairman, Calista Corporation Board of Directors; tribal government official (Yup'ik)

Lerner Publications Company
A division of Lerner Publishing Group, Inc.
241 First Avenue North
Minneapolis, MN 55401 USA

For reading levels and more information, look up this title at www.lernerbooks.com.

Main body text set in Rockwell Std Light 12/16.
Typeface provided by Monotype Typography.

Library of Congress Cataloging-in-Publication Data

Names: Kallen, Stuart A., 1955– author.
Title: Native peoples of the Subarctic / Stuart Kallen.
Description: Minneapolis : Lerner Publications, 2017. | Series: North american indian nations | Includes bibliographical references and index.
Identifiers: LCCN 2015051187 (print) | LCCN 2015051370 (ebook) | ISBN 9781467779388 (lb : alk. paper) | ISBN 9781512412444 (pb : alk. paper) | ISBN 9781512410778 (eb pdf)
Subjects: LCSH: Inuit—Arctic regions—History—Juvenile literature. | Inuit—Arctic regions—Social life and customs—Juvenile literature. | Indians of North America--Arctic regions—History—Juvenile literature. | Indians of North America—Arctic regions—Social life and customs—Juvenile literature.
Classification: LCC E99.E7 K127 2017 (print) | LCC E99.E7 (ebook) | DDC 970.004/9712—dc23

LC record available at http://lccn.loc.gov/2015051187

Manufactured in the United States of America
1-37529-18674-3/23/2016

CONTENTS

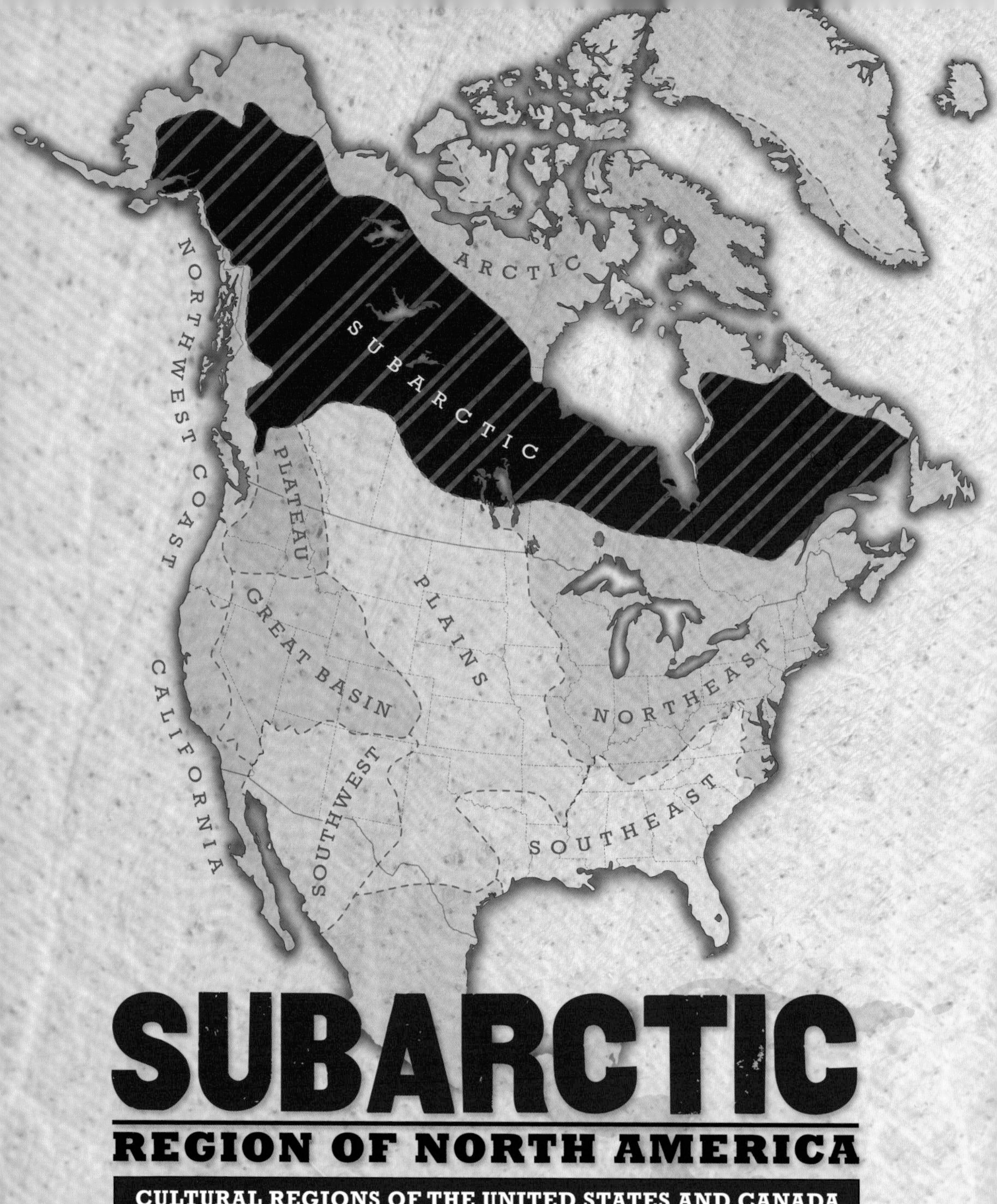

SUBARCTIC

REGION OF NORTH AMERICA

CULTURAL REGIONS OF THE UNITED STATES AND CANADA

- Plateau
- Northwest Coast
- California
- Plains
- Southeast
- Southwest
- Great Basin
- Northeast
- Subarctic
- Arctic
- Other
- Cultural area border
- International border
- State/province border

INTRODUCTION

Long before humans walked the earth, there were only giant animals. One day the creator god Great Raven, or Dotson' Sa, told his son Raven to make a huge boat. Raven worked hard to make the boat. When the boat was finished, rain began to fall. All the animals came onto the boat in pairs. Soon the whole world flooded. Only the animals on the boat survived.

When the flood began to die down, a giant muskrat jumped off Raven's boat. He swam down to the ocean floor. Muskrat used his tail to stir up mud. He piled the dirt until land appeared. Then Dotson' Sa made rivers, lakes, trees, plants, and berries. He decided to make creatures too. He made a man and a woman from clay. The couple married and had children who filled the land.

This is the story that Athabascan (a-thuh-BAS-ken) peoples tell about how the world came to be. The Athabascan are native peoples who live in a region of North America called the Subarctic. The Subarctic covers much of Canada and Alaska. It begins 1,600 miles (2,575 kilometers) below the North Pole at the Arctic Circle. The region stretches about 1,400 miles (2,253 km) to the south. Average winter temperatures in the subarctic can range from 30°F to −65°F (−1°C to −53°C). There can be

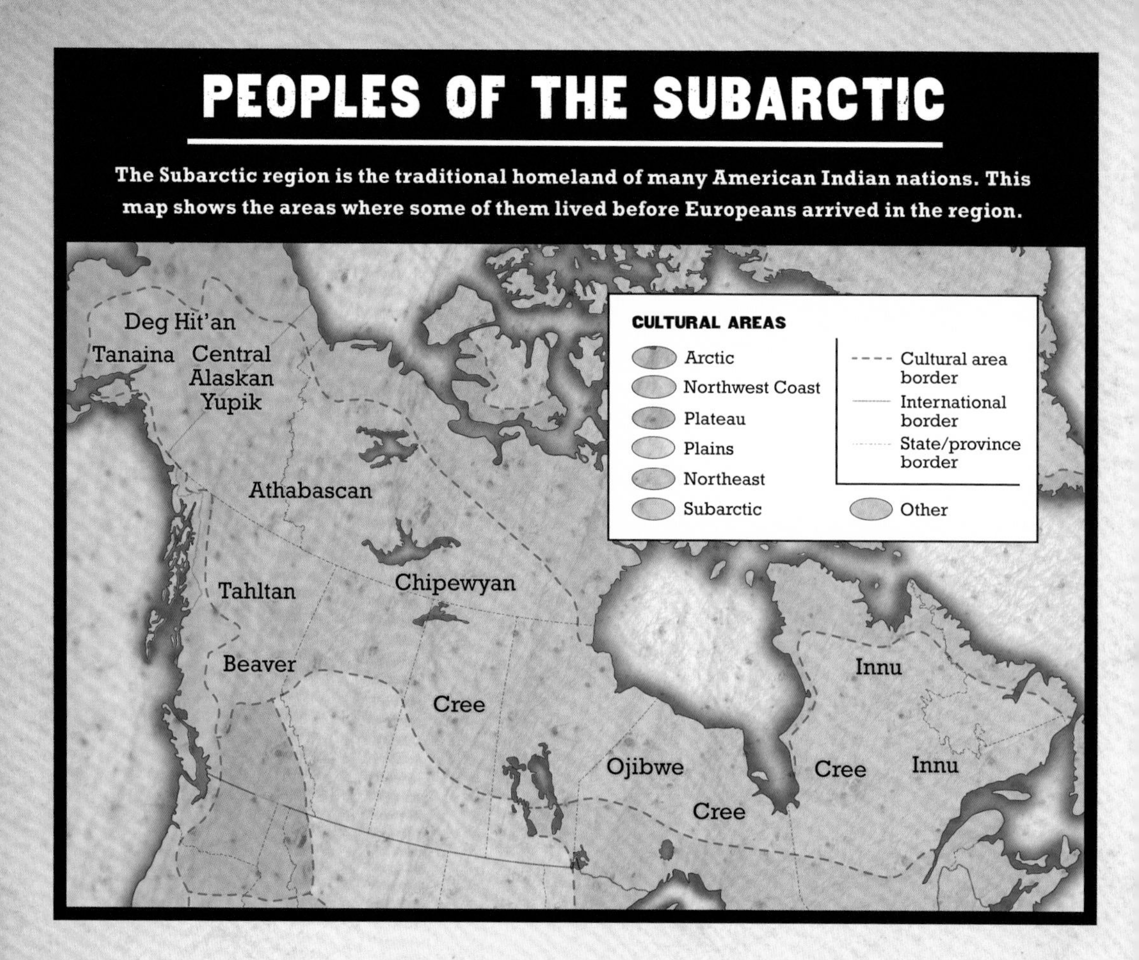

PEOPLES OF THE SUBARCTIC

The Subarctic region is the traditional homeland of many American Indian nations. This map shows the areas where some of them lived before Europeans arrived in the region.

snow on the ground two hundred days a year.

Thousands of native peoples call the Subarctic home. Native peoples who live in Canada are called First Nations peoples. Subarctic peoples in Alaska are known as Alaska Natives. These native peoples speak several different languages that come from a few main language groups.

First Nations peoples who live east of the Churchill River in northern Manitoba, Canada, speak languages from the Algonquian (al-GAHN-kwee-an) language group. These nations include the Ojibwe (oh-JIB-way), several groups of Cree (KREE), and the Innu (IN-yoo). Nations west of the Churchill speak Athabascan (also spelled Athapaskan or Athabaskan) languages. These nations include the Chipewyan (chip-uh-WY-an), Beaver, Tahltan (TAHL-ten), Tanaina (ta-nay-EYE-na), and Deg Hit'an (degg-HEET-an). The Central Alaskan Yup'ik (YOO-puhk) who live in the Subarctic regions of western, central, and southwestern Alaska speak a language from the Eskimo-Aleut (ES-kih-moh-AH-lee-yoot) language group. The Yup'ik are culturally distinct from other Subarctic nations. They are related to Inuit and are often considered to be an Arctic nation. But many Yup'ik practices are also similar to those of other Subarctic peoples.

The Subarctic region covers much of Alaska and Canada below the Arctic Circle.

Black bears were one of many kinds of animals hunted across the Subarctic.

Hunting and Fishing

The native peoples of the Subarctic have depended on nature for centuries. Those who lived near the ocean hunted seals, walruses, and whales. Nations that lived in the forest hunted black bears, lynx, caribou, beavers, gray wolves, red foxes, river otters, and snowshoe hare. Subarctic peoples also depended on the fish and waterfowl found in the many lakes, rivers, and ponds.

The Modern Subarctic

Most Subarctic peoples live like other North Americans. They drive cars, snowmobiles, and motorboats. They live in heated homes, watch television, and use the Internet. But many native peoples continue to practice their cultural traditions. They might

NATIONS, LANGUAGES, AND REGIONS

SUBARCTIC NATION	OTHER NAMES OR RELATED NATIONS	LANGUAGE GROUP	REGION
Beaver	Dane-zaa	Athabascan	Peace River, Alberta
Chipewyan	Dene, Denesuline	Athabascan	Manitoba, Alberta, and Saskatchewan
Cree	Innu, Plains Cree, Woods Cree	Algonquian	Manitoba, Alberta, and Saskatchewan
Ojibwe	Ojibway, Ojibwa, Anishinaabe, Chippewa	Algonquian	Ontario and Manitoba
Tahltan	Tagish, Tlingit	Athabascan	Telegraph Creek, British Columbia
Yup'ik	Central Alaskan Yup'ik	Eskimo-Aleut	Alaska

shop in grocery stores, but they also hunt and fish as their ancestors did.

As long as the snow, cold, and wind have ruled the northern forests, the native peoples of the Subarctic have thrived. Different nations speak different languages, live in different areas, and have different practices. But the native peoples of the Subarctic also share a common history and way of life.

CHAPTER 1

SURVIVAL THROUGH THE SEASONS

Subarctic nations had close ties to the land, water, and animals. These ties helped them survive the harsh climate. Subarctic peoples were in tune with the changing seasons too. The long winter was followed by a very short spring when ice melted along rivers, lakes, and ocean shores. The summer lasted only a few months. But the weather could be warm, humid, and rainy. In the fall, the weather quickly turned snowy and cold. Each season provided a chance to hunt, fish, and gather food in different places.

Birds, Fish, and Greens

In central Alaska, the Yup'ik word for April means "Bird Place." During this month, millions of birds nested and mated in the wetlands. The lakes and ponds filled with geese, ducks, cranes, and seabirds. Yup'ik men hunted them with bows and arrows. Boys as young as eight could test their hunting skills too.

Women and young girls were also very busy. They harvested eggs from the birds' nests. They filled baskets with wild parsnips and wild celery. In the coastal regions, they dug for clams and mussels at low tide.

When fishing season began in June, the riverbanks buzzed with activity. The Yup'ik called the Yukon River Kwikpak (kwee-PUCK). This means "Great River, Provider for All and Why We Live." The name relates to the amount of fish found in the river. Salmon were especially common. The Yukon waters were also full of whitefish, smelt, and pike. These fish fed the Yup'ik year-round.

In April, Yup'ik men and women hunted and collected eggs from the many birds that nested in the wetlands.

The Yup'ik caught fish using nets, spears, and fishing poles with bone fishhooks. One popular fishing method used a V-shaped fence of poles called a weir. The weir was placed in the stream. As the salmon swam upstream to reproduce, or spawn, they would try to jump over the weir. When the fish jumped out of the water, teenage boys and girls killed them with special salmon clubs.

Some salmon was eaten fresh. Extra fish were dried in the sun and stored for the winter. Yup'ik women used the salmon skin to make waterproof parkas, mittens, and boots.

Moose in a Lake

In September, the Chipewyan and Northern Ojibwe would begin hunting moose. Moose can be nearly 7 feet (2 meters) tall at the

The many rivers across the Subarctic provided fish and allowed Subarctic peoples to more easily hunt moose.

SUBARCTIC CLOTHING

Warm, waterproof clothing was important for surviving in the Subarctic. Women made clothing for their families. They sewed clothing with needles made from animal bones and tusks. In the northern forests, native peoples wore moccasins, leggings, and coats made from soft, tanned hides of caribou and moose. Western Athabascan peoples wore shirts decorated with dyed porcupine quills and beads made from seeds. In winter, Athabascan men and women wore pants with moccasins attached and a long coat with a belted waist. They wore a separate hood or hat and mittens. At night, they wore sleeping robes. These were made from rabbit skins that were cut into strips and woven together.

shoulder and weigh more than 1,000 pounds (453 kilograms). Their size makes them hard to hunt on land. But moose often swim, so Subarctic native peoples could hunt them from canoes. When a hunter saw a moose swimming in a lake, he would paddle near the animal and try to spear it. If this did not work, the hunter might jump onto the animal's back. He would then cut its throat with a bone knife. The dead moose would be towed to shore with a rope attached to the canoe.

At the camp, women butchered the moose. They cooked the meat into a stew using stone boilers. These were waterproof baskets made from pieces of birch bark. Hot stones were dropped in the bark pots to heat the food. Moose meat was also turned into a food called pemmican. Pemmican was a nutritious food that could be preserved for years and carried long distances by hunters. It was eaten raw, boiled, or fried. To make

Pemmican was made from dried meat, animal fat, and berries. It was easy for hunters to carry with them on long trips, and it provided plenty of energy.

pemmican, women dried thin slices of meat over a low fire. They used rocks to pound the dried meat into tiny pieces. Then they mixed the meat with melted animal fat and dried berries.

Shelter

During fishing and hunting season, Subarctic native peoples moved from place to place. They lived in small shelters that were easy to set up and take down. The Chipewyan, Ojibwe, and Athabascan peoples lived in small cone-shaped tents called tipis. They made these tents from animal skins and pine trees called lodgepoles. A fire was built in the center of a tipi, and smoke rose out of a hole at the top. Tipi floors were covered with animal skins. Skins were also used for blankets.

For the winter, Subarctic native peoples built sturdier shelters that were partly underground. To build one of these shelters, a hole was dug in the ground and logs were laid on top of one another to form the walls. Spaces between the logs were filled with mud, moss, and brush. Walls might also be covered with a thick layer of grass and dirt called sod. Animal skins on the insides of the walls added an extra layer to keep families warm.

Many Subarctic nations lived in tipis similar to this Cree shelter.

CHAPTER 2

FAMILY, SPIRITS, AND LEGENDS

People in the Subarctic needed to work together to survive the extreme temperatures. This meant that families were very important for native peoples of the Subarctic. A typical Subarctic group might consist of one hundred members from twenty families. These small bands had unofficial leaders. The leaders were often the best hunters or the wisest members of the group. Each band belonged to a larger group. These groups shared the same language but claimed their own territories. In the summer, the bands gathered in groups of up to one thousand people. They held large hunts, played games, and performed ceremonies.

Families

During summer celebrations, parents arranged marriages for their children. Girls married when they were about thirteen years old. Boys married at about the age of seventeen. The couple moved in with the girl's family after the ceremony. When a boy could hunt well enough to support his wife, the couple set out to live on their own. But they did not go too far. Everyone

Children often worked with adults to perform tasks necessary for survival, such as hunting and cooking. Passing skills to the next generation has always been an important part of the lives of native Subarctic peoples.

needed to work together to make sure the group could survive. Families often came together to hunt, fish, and socialize.

Children had to work as hard as adults. Boys as young as seven learned how to paddle kayaks, shoot arrows, and throw harpoons. Young girls helped butcher animals, clean fish, and dry meat. Mothers taught their daughters to sew, gather wild foods, preserve food, and cook for the family.

The Powers of Spirits

Almost every daily activity was governed by spirits. Subarctic peoples believed that spirits gave life to rocks, trees, storms, mountains, and rivers. Spirits ruled seals, salmon, moose, caribou, bears, and other animals. The most important spirits were those of dead ancestors. These spirits might appear in dreams to give advice.

Spirits could be helpful or harmful. A spirit could bring luck to a hunt. But an angry spirit might send animals far from a hunter's camp. Evil spirits could bring sickness. They could also be asked to hurt an enemy. Subarctic native peoples viewed spirits with a mix of love, respect, and fear.

The Yup'ik Way of Life

The Yup'ik referred to their spirituality as the Way of Life. They respected all living things. For example, if bears were scarce, the hunter did not become upset with the animals no matter how great his hunger. Instead, he prayed to the bear spirit and

Bears were important to the Yup'ik Way of Life. The Yup'ik learned to respect both bears and the bear spirit.

offered his devotion. If a bear was killed, the hunter thanked the animal for giving the gift of its life. After a successful hunt, the Way of Life said that the bear skull should be brought inside and treated as a respected guest. For three days, the hunter gave the skull small food offerings so there would be many bears to hunt in the future.

The Wendigo

One of the most fearsome spirits of the north woods was the phantom of starvation known as the Wendigo. This spirit often appeared at the end of winter. During this time, Cree and Ojibwe peoples rarely left their shelters even as they ran out of food.

As the native peoples starved, the giant Wendigo walked through the land. The monster had bulging eyes; a lipless mouth; long, jagged teeth; and a heart of ice. The Wendigo preyed on the weak, the sick, and the hungry. If a hunter left his shelter to find a rabbit or squirrel to eat, the Wendigo stalked the hunter.

According to Ojibwe legend, the Wendigo was once a hunter. One very cold winter, there was no game to be found. The hunter starved. He prayed to evil spirits for help. The man fell asleep, and when he awoke, he was the Wendigo. The evil spirits had answered his prayers. He now had magical powers.

The Wendigo walked through the snow until he came upon an Ojibwe village. He gave three terrifying shouts. The villagers fainted in fear. And the Wendigo used his powers to turn the people to beavers. The Wendigo ate them and grew taller than the treetops. Soon his head was in the clouds. But as he grew, he also got hungrier. Soon the Wendigo ate all the beavers and all the fish. He left the people to starve. Whenever people ran out of food, they feared the Wendigo was nearby.

THE SHAKING TENT

Shamans who lived among the Ojibwe, Innu, and Cree performed a special ritual called the shaking tent ceremony. The ritual was held for someone who was sick or troubled by evil spirits. Before the ceremony, the person built a round, barrel-shaped tent from saplings and animal skins. The shaman would begin singing, drumming, and praying. Then the person would enter the tent. The people believed that during the ritual, spirits would arrive at the tent. The spirits would make the tent shake wildly. Sometimes small sparks like stars might fly around the tent. The shaman asked for blessings for the person in the tent. Then the air would fill with loud spirit voices. The ceremony ended at dawn. Then the person would be healed or cured of his or her troubles.

Ojibwe men in Canada constructing a shaking tent

Shamans

The legend of the Wendigo warned people that they should never call on the evil spirits. It was better to call on those with good powers. These people were known as shamans, medicine men, medicine women, or priests and priestesses.

When shamans held ceremonies, they sang, danced, drummed, and prayed for hours. This helped them to enter a trance. In this dreamlike state, shamans traveled to the spirit world and communicated with the spirits.

Shamans called on the spirits for success during hunts and victory in war. Shamans looked into the future to predict the weather or the movement of caribou herds. When someone was sick, the shaman worked with healing spirits to heal the person's soul. Sometimes, the spirits gave recipes for medicine that could be made from herbs and plants.

Shamans were thought to have special powers. But all Subarctic natives could speak to the spirits. They knew they had little control over their harsh world. To survive, they had to respect the spirits of nature.

CHAPTER 3

ART, SONG, AND DANCE

Spirits provided food, strength, and health. They also inspired artists, singers, and dancers. Images of spirits were painted on rocks, carved into statues and masks, and stitched into clothing. The words to the songs of the shamans were said to be brought forth by spirits. Stories about spirits were acted out in dances and rituals.

Ancient Rock Art

Some of the oldest art in North America consists of symbols called pictographs. These symbols were painted onto rocks by Subarctic native peoples. There are more than five hundred pictograph sites between Quebec and northern Saskatchewan. Each site features many pictographs.

Rock paintings in northwestern Ontario can be two thousand to five thousand years old. The symbols were made with black, white, or yellow dye or a red mineral-based paint called ocher. Subarctic peoples typically painted with their fingers. But sometimes they painted with paintbrushes made of animal or plant fibers.

The rock art depicts humans, animals, and spirits from ancient legends. The Horned Serpent is one mythical creature in the paintings. This creature was a reptile spirit. It lurked in lakes and rivers and attacked people in canoes. The mythical Thunderbird is also in many Subarctic pictographs. The Thunderbird was responsible for rain, thunder, and lightning. Some rock paintings show the Thunderbird killing its enemy, the Horned Serpent, with lightning bolts.

This pictograph is believed to have been painted by an Ojibwe shaman.

THE THUNDERBIRD

The Thunderbird is one of the few creatures from indigenous mythology that is common among nations in many regions. Northeast and Northwest peoples as well as peoples of the Canadian Subarctic tell legends of the Thunderbird. The Thunderbird is said to have magical powers and amazing strength. When the creature flaps its wings, it produces thunder. When the Thunderbird blinks its eyes, lightning bolts shoot out.

The Thunderbird is shown as a large raptor, or bird of prey, like the bald eagle. The creature has huge wings, curling horns, a long beak, and a bald head. The Cree believed that thunderstorms were a contest between the Thunderbird and a huge snake called the Horned Serpent. Anyone who survived a lightning strike was said to receive the Thunderbird's spirit powers. These people often became shamans.

The Mask Dance

This Deg Hit'an mask represents a mythical creature. It would have been worn in ceremonial dances.

Carved masks were important to the spiritual life of the Subarctic native peoples. Each spring, the Deg Hit'an performed the mask dance to honor the animal spirits. The dance was held to inspire the spirits to send animals to the hunters in the coming year.

To prepare for the mask dance, the Deg Hit'an made masks of the spirits of salmon, caribou, grouse, foxes, ravens, and humanlike creatures. If a hunter had a dream about an animal, he would carve it into a mask. Some images mixed features from a few different creatures. The carved masks might be painted and decorated with fur, feathers, or bones. The masks were said to make the unseen world visible.

People wearing masks visited nearby villages to invite their neighbors to join the ceremony. When guests arrived, they were brought to a lodge called a *kashim*. These houses were used as community centers for men year-round. Men and boys lived, worked, ate, bathed, and slept in the kashim.

During the mask dance, everyone gathered at the kashim. Men and women both danced. But only the men could wear masks. The mask dance was a serious event. But the dances might also involve humor. For example, during the grouse dance, dancers imitated the spinning and leg-shaking movements of the grouse.

Spirit Land Songs

Sometimes Deg Hit'an carvers wrote songs to go with their masks. Spirit songs were also important to the Beaver people who lived in what is now Alberta, Canada.

Shamans of the Beaver nation sometimes danced and drummed for so long that they collapsed into a deathlike trance. In this state, the souls of the shamans were said to fly like swans to the spirit land beyond the sky. While in the heavenly realm, the shamans learned songs from the spirits. When they awoke, they shared these songs with the rest of the people.

Harmony and Joy

Subarctic peoples wrote songs about traveling, love, war, mourning, and happiness. Music was a part of their everyday lives. Among the Cree, songs were an important part of hunting. Through songs, hunters might ask the spirits for a good hunt. The songs might also be seen as bringing animals to the hunter. These songs reflected the rhythms of nature. They helped the hunters connect with both the spirits and the animals.

Among Cree and Ojibwe, music was also an important part of healing. Each plant and medicine had its own song to go with it. For the Ojibwe, song and dance were almost inseparable. To ask the spirits for healing, they would sing and dance. Music helped the people connect with one another and with the spirits.

Often drummers played along with these songs. They used wooden sticks and round, handheld drums. Another common instrument among Subarctic peoples was the fiddle. The fiddle was introduced to Subarctic natives by outsiders. But they soon developed their own unique music and dances using the fiddle.

Making music and art was important to Subarctic peoples. The arts honored the spirits. They also provided relief from boredom during the winters. In warmer months, the arts brought people together. Song, dance, and art added joy to the hard work of daily survival.

Music was an important part of Subarctic culture. This Cree drum was played during an environmental protest in Montreal, Quebec.

CHAPTER 4

THE EUROPEAN AND AMERICAN ERAS

In May 1534, the French explorer Jacques Cartier sailed along the coast of present-day Labrador in northeastern Canada. The explorer could not believe that anyone could live in the region. Cartier wrote that the land was made of "stones and horrible rugged rocks. . . . I did not see one cartload of earth and yet I landed in many places . . . there is nothing but moss and short, stunted shrub."

The French explorer Jacques Cartier first came to what is now Canada in 1534.

Algonquian-speaking First Nations peoples were there to greet Cartier and his crew of sailors. They were eager to trade beaver furs for the glass beads, red sailor hats, and iron knives the French carried on their ship.

The French Fur Trade

Cartier soon went home with a load of beaver pelts. He sold them to French hatmakers who valued the fur because it could be shaped into stylish hats. By the mid-sixteenth century, the demand for beaver hats in Europe sparked a fur rush. Dozens of French ships sailed to what is now Canada each summer to get beaver pelts from the Subarctic peoples. By the seventeenth century, thousands of Europeans were moving to Canada to be part of the fur trade.

In 1608, the French explorer Samuel de Champlain founded the city of Quebec on the Saint Lawrence River. From here, the French set up a network of trading posts that would one day stretch across the Subarctic from the Atlantic Ocean to the Pacific.

Beaver pelts from Canada were in high demand by Europeans who wore hats made from the fur.

Impact of the Fur Trade

The fur trade depended on the hunting and trapping skills of First Nations peoples. First Nations peoples provided furs for trading. They also showed the French how to survive in the wilderness. They taught the traders how to make canoes and snowshoes, where to find food, and how to find shelter in the cold.

The French provided the First Nations peoples with wool blankets, guns, metal knives, tools, sewing needles, and pots and pans. These items made life easier for the Subarctic native peoples. But they also got in the way of ancient traditions. Subarctic hunters began using guns. They stopped making knives and arrowheads from stones. Women who cooked with cast iron pans no longer made stone boilers from birch bark.

The First Nations peoples came to depend on European items for survival. But the beaver was hunted almost to extinction. The Subarctic peoples could not rely on the fur trade. When the beavers were wiped out in one region, the fur traders moved on. They left the First Nations peoples behind with nothing to trade. This could be deadly. During winter, Subarctic peoples sometimes died of hunger because they had no gunpowder or ammunition for their muskets.

Beavers were hunted almost to extinction, leaving First Nations peoples with nothing to trade.

The fur trade had another serious impact on First Nations peoples. The French carried European diseases such as smallpox, measles, and the flu. Subarctic peoples had no natural immunity to these deadly diseases. A flu epidemic swept across the Subarctic in 1740. Thousands of First Nations peoples died. In 1780, a smallpox epidemic killed about half of the Cree, Northern Ojibwe, and Chipewyan.

The Russian Hunters

Subarctic Alaska Natives faced the same problems as nations to the east. Russian fur traders came to the region in the 1810s. In 1818, a Russian trader named Petr Korsakovski built the first European trading post. It was on Bristol Bay in Southwest Alaska. A fur business called the Russian-American Company (RAC) came to the region too.

Subarctic hunters helped the Russians obtain millions of furs. In 1821, a list of furs purchased by the RAC included 1.3 million fox, 73,000 sea otter, and 31,000 sable pelts. They also got thousands of pelts from lynx, wolves, walruses, and bears.

Like the First Nations peoples, Alaska Natives came to depend on Russian trade goods for survival. Animals hunted for fur were nearly wiped out. And disease was also a problem. A smallpox outbreak in 1838 killed about 60 percent of the Yup'ik population.

By the end of the nineteenth century, the lives of Subarctic native peoples were forever changed. The animals the native peoples had relied upon for centuries were becoming scarce. Families were torn apart by poverty and disease. And the ancient traditions of Subarctic peoples were nearly forgotten.

CHAPTER 5

MODERN TIMES

During the nineteenth century, white Americans from the United States were a common sight in the western Subarctic. The outsiders came in the summer to trade furs. In September, they sailed south to warmer regions. But in 1896, gold was discovered in the Klondike region of the Yukon Territory in Canada. Two years later, gold was found near Nome, Alaska. These discoveries started a gold rush. More than one hundred thousand hopeful miners came to the Yukon and Alaska.

The discovery of gold in the Yukon Territory started the Klondike gold rush.

Some local Subarctic native peoples profited from the gold trade. Men worked as packers. They carried loads of

Miners in Alaska during the Klondike gold rush

up to 100 pounds (45 kg) of supplies along winding mountain trails. The work was hard, but it paid better than hunting or trapping. Other native peoples worked as guides, cooks, cleaners, woodcutters, and deckhands on ships.

Like the fur trade, the gold rush was both good and bad for Subarctic native peoples. Some moved away from their families into gold camps. In the camps, they were exposed to disease, violence, alcohol, and crime. And like the fur trade, the gold rush did not provide steady work. By 1910, the rush had ended.

"Overrun with White People"

After the gold rush, many outsiders stayed in the region and founded small towns. The newcomers wanted the US government to build a railroad to connect their towns to the coast. A railroad would open up new lands for Euro-American settlement. It would also provide jobs for residents.

In 1914, funds were approved to build an all-weather railroad. The route would stretch 470 miles (756 km) from the interior town of Fairbanks to the coast city of Seward. When people in Fairbanks heard the news, church bells rang, and people cheered in the streets. But the Alaska Natives in the region were not happy. The rail line would cut through Tanaina lands.

The Tanaina feared the railroad would bring Euro-Americans who would take all the best land. Thomas Riggs Jr., who was in charge of building the Alaska Railroad, agreed. He warned the Tanaina that their lands would soon be "overrun with white people who would kill off your game, your moose, your caribou, and your sheep. They will run them all out of the country and they will have so many [fishermen] on the river that the Indian will not get as many fish." Riggs and other government officials wanted to give the Alaska Natives the chance to own the land before it was taken by Euro-Americans.

For the first time in Alaska, Alaska Natives and nonnative US government officials gathered in 1915 to discuss land use. Alaska Native chiefs told the government that they did not want to be placed on reservations. They wanted to remain free. They chose instead to receive individual plots of land. The government also promised that white Americans would not be able to take land that was part of an Alaska Native village.

The Alaska Railroad had mixed results for Alaska Natives. It brought white settlers who cleared the land and built farms

Thomas Riggs Jr. warned Alaska Natives that their lands would likely be taken over by white Americans when the railroad was built.

on what had once been Tanaina land. Native hunting and fishing areas became smaller. Some people were forced to move to cities to find work. But some Tanaina found permanent jobs working for the railroad. And trains delivered goods such as furniture, tools, and clothing to the Alaska Natives for the first time.

Giving Up Traditional Ways

Outsiders continued to move into Subarctic Canada throughout the twentieth century. The Canadian government passed laws that forced First Nations peoples to give up their traditional ways. Ancient hunting and fishing grounds were sold to white settlers. In Alberta and Saskatchewan, First Nations peoples were given small plots of land to farm. Some became successful farmers. But many failed and were left in poverty. They had no way to support themselves. In the Northwest Territories in Canada, laws kept First Nations peoples from leaving their lands without permission from government agents.

First Nations leaders spoke out against these government policies. In 1930, Canada changed its laws. First Nations peoples were given the right to hunt, trap, and fish for food on all unoccupied lands. But Canadian development continued to disrupt native life. The Canadian government built highways, railroads, airports, and oil pipelines throughout the Subarctic. First Nations peoples helped with these projects. But they were often left without jobs when the projects were completed.

Relearning the Old Ways

During much of the twentieth century, Subarctic native children were sent to schools where they were taught in English. Christian churches taught them Christianity. Many native peoples stopped practicing the ways of traditional shamans.

By the early twenty-first century, some feared that Subarctic native traditions were disappearing. These native peoples began working to preserve their cultures. Elders began sharing their wisdom with young people. In the Innu nation, a website called Nametau Innu was started as a way for elders to pass on knowledge and skills to the younger generation. Subarctic native teachers are also working to revive native languages and teach students traditional dances and songs. Since 1985, the Innu have held the Innu Nikamu festival each summer. The

Subarctic native teachers and elders are working to ensure that their cultures and languages stay alive. This student in Quebec is learning the Cree language.

festival showcases First Nations music and culture. Members of the Ojibwe Nation continue to practice many of their traditional ceremonies and dances too. These actions have helped a generation of Subarctic native peoples to discover their rich cultural heritage.

Fighting for Rights

Many Subarctic peoples are also working to protect Subarctic lands and get better treatment from the US and Canadian governments. Many Innu and Cree have set up organizations to fight for the rights of First Nations peoples. Some nations have

A worker with the Pebble Mine project drills in the Bristol Bay region of Alaska.

achieved the ability to govern themselves. Others have been able to settle land claims or receive help from government programs.

In 2002, a Canadian company called Northern Dynasty Minerals wanted to build the Pebble Mine in a remote region of Alaska. The project would involve digging the largest open-pit mine in North America. The company hoped to reach gold valued at $120 billion.

But Yup'ik in the region were against the Pebble Mine. The mine would interfere with their hunting and fishing lands. It would release toxic wastewater into the salmon habitat. In 2014, the Yup'ik protesters were successful. The United States

YUP'IK ELDER BOBBY ANDREW

Yup'ik elder Bobby Andrew led the protests against the Pebble Mine in Alaska. Born in 1943, Andrew spent most of his life as a hunter and fisherman. When plans went forward for the mine in 2002, Andrew feared the operation would harm the ancient salmon fisheries in the area. Andrew worked to stop the mine. He attended hearings in Alaska and Washington, DC. He talked to politicians and businesses. Shortly before his death in 2015 at the age of seventy-two, the EPA stopped the project from going forward. Many credit Andrew for putting a halt to the Pebble Mine.

Many people in Alaska joined Bobby Andrew in protesting the Pebble Mine in Bristol Bay.

Environmental Protection Agency ruled against the project.

Another movement began in 2012. Four women in Saskatchewan, Canada, began talking about a government bill that would interfere with First Nations land. They held an event called Idle No More to teach the community about the bill. After this event, Idle No More became a national movement. First Nations leaders asked the government to remove the bill. First Nations peoples across Canada held dances and marches at malls. One Cree chief even refused to eat until the government agreed to meet with First Nations leaders. Eventually, Idle No More encouraged native peoples in the United States and around the world to speak up for their rights and to protect their lands too.

Cree Chief Theresa Spence *(above)* went on a six-week hunger strike in 2012. Her strike ended after First Nations leaders and members of the Canadian government signed a declaration in support of aboriginal issues.

SUBARCTIC POPULATIONS

SUBARCTIC NATION	APPROXIMATE CURRENT POPULATION
Beaver	3,000
Chipewyan	22,750
Cree	More than 200,000
Innu	22,000
Ojibwe	163,500
Tahltan	1,500
Yup'ik	34,000

* Population numbers as of 2014 data

A Foot in Both Worlds

About 110,000 native peoples live in Alaska. Many of them live in the Subarctic. About 1.4 million First Nations peoples from six hundred nations live in Canada. The last two centuries have brought many changes for these peoples. But they have adapted to these changes in order to thrive. Subarctic nations continue to practice their traditional ways and honor the wisdom of their ancestors while living modern lives.

NOTABLE SUBARCTIC NATIVE PEOPLE

Josephine Bacon (Innu)
is a poet, songwriter, and documentary filmmaker from Quebec, Canada. She writes poetry in both French and Innu-aimun, the language of her ancestors. Her work tells the stories of Innu elders, reflects on the connection of her people to their lands, and explores the changing environments and languages of the Innu people.

Adam Beach (Ojibwe)
is an actor who was born on the Dog Creek Lake Reserve in Manitoba, Canada. He was cast in his first role at the age of sixteen and went on to appear in more than sixty movies and TV shows. He has had major roles in *Squanto: A Warrior's Tale, Smoke Signals, Windtalkers,* and *Flags of Our Fathers.*

Alano Edzerza (Tahltan)
won his first award for sculpture in 1994 at the age of thirteen. Edzerza's early talent developed into a professional career with gallery and museum shows around the world. His works use traditional regional themes and images such as whales, eagles, and spirits like the Raven.

Buffy Sainte-Marie (Cree)
is a Canadian singer-songwriter born on the Piapot Cree Reserve in Saskatchewan, Canada. She became a popular folksinger in the 1960s and became an activist for First Nations rights in the following decades. Sainte-Marie's 2015 album *Power in the Blood* won Canada's Polaris Music Prize.

Timeline:

Each Subarctic nation had its own way of recording history. This timeline is based on the Gregorian calendar, which Europeans brought to the Subarctic.

9000 BCE Native peoples arrive in the Subarctic regions.

1534 French explorer Jacques Cartier is the first European to describe and map the Subarctic regions of eastern Canada.

1608 French explorer Samuel de Champlain founds the city of Quebec on the Saint Lawrence River in Canada.

1818 Russian fur trader Petr Korsakovski builds the first European trading post on Bristol Bay in Alaska.

1838 A smallpox epidemic kills 60 percent of the Yup'ik population in Alaska.

1867 The United States purchases Alaska from Russia.

1896 Gold is discovered in the Klondike region of the Yukon, which brings tens of thousands of gold seekers to the region.

1898 A second gold rush begins when gold is discovered around Nome, Alaska.

1914 US Congress approves the construction of the Alaska Railroad from Fairbanks to Seward.

1959 On January 3, Alaska becomes the forty-ninth state.

2002 Exploration begins at the Pebble Mine site in the Bristol Bay watershed in Alaska.

2014 Under pressure from Yup'ik leaders and other environmentalists, the Environmental Protection Agency prohibits the Pebble Mine project.

Glossary

ancestor: a blood relative from whom one is descended

band: a subgroup of a nation

bill: a draft of a law presented to the government for consideration

Euro-American: someone living in the United States who is of European descent

First Nations: the term used to describe the 617 First Nation communities in Canada

grouse: a bird that lives on the ground and has feathers on its legs

indigenous: descended from the original occupants of a land before the land was taken over by others

language group: languages related to one another and sharing common roots

parka: a warm coat with a hood

pelt: the skin of an animal with the fur still on it

pictographs: painted symbols that represent animals, spirits, or words

preserve: to keep something in its original state or in good condition

reservation: an area of land in the United States specially set aside for American Indians to live on.

trance: a dreamlike state between sleeping and waking that may be achieved by hours of dancing, drumming, and singing

Source Notes

28 Jacques Cartier, *The Voyages of Jacques Cartier* (Toronto: University of Toronto Press, 1993), 10.

34 "Interior Alaska 1901–1950," Alaska History & Cultural Studies, accessed February 15, 2016, http://www.akhistorycourse.org/articles/article.php?artID=60.

Selected Bibliography

Grinev, Andrei Val'terovich. *The Tlingit Indians in Russian America, 1741–1867.* Lincoln: University of Nebraska, 2005.

Jolles, Carol Zane. *Faith, Food, and Family in a Yupik Whaling Community.* Seattle: University of Washington Press, 2002.

Symons, R. D. *The First People.* Saskatoon, Saskatchewan: Western Producer Prairie Books, 1978.

Williams, Maria Sháa Tláa, ed. *The Alaska Native Reader.* Durham, NC: Duke University Press, 2011.

Further Information

Alaska History & Cultural Studies
http://www.akhistorycourse.org
This comprehensive site covers Alaska geography, culture, and history including rich details about native life and the Russian and American eras.

Heritage: Newfoundland and Labrador
http://www.heritage.nf.ca/index.php
Read more about the culture of the Innu as well as the history of Labrador and its other First Nations peoples.

Kallen, Stuart A. *Native Peoples of the Arctic.* Minneapolis: Lerner Publications, 2017. This book explores traditions and customs, history, and the modern-day lives of native peoples who live north of the Arctic Circle.

Kuiper, Kathleen, *Indigenous Peoples of the Arctic, Subarctic, and Northwest Coast.* New York: Rosen, 2012. This book looks at the histories, lifestyles, and the spiritual and cultural traditions of the indigenous peoples of northern regions.

Loyie, Larry. *As Long as the Rivers Flow.* Toronto: Douglas & McIntyre, 2005. This book, written by a native Cree, tells the story of a young boy's last summer at home before being taken to a residential school.

Subarctic People
http://firstpeoplesofcanada.com/fp_groups/fp_subarctic1.html
Learn more about the Subarctic native peoples in Canada, including information about numerous bands and their traditions, art, spirituality, trade and travel, history, and modern lives.

30 Fascinating Facts about the Boreal Forest
http://www.treehugger.com/natural-sciences/30-fascinating-facts-about-the-boreal-forest.html
The facts, figures, and pictures on this website provide insight into the ecological zone that represents nearly one-third of Earth's forest cover.

Index

Photo Acknowledgments

The images in this book are used with the permission of: © iStockphoto.com/Bastar (paper background); © Dave Kuebler/Thinkstock, pp. 2–3; © Laura Westlund/Independent Picture Service, pp. 4, 6; © Ron Niebrugge/Alamy, p. 7; © Design Pics Inc/Alamy, pp. 8, 11 © iStockphoto.com/eyebex, p. 12; © Jenn Arr/Wikimedia Commons (Creative Commons Attribution 2.0 Generic license), p. 14; © SuperStock, p. 15; © Megapress/Alamy, pp. 17, 27, 29; © All Canada Photos/Alamy, pp. 18, 30; American Philosophical Society, p. 20; © Thomas Kitchin & Victoria Hurst/All Canada Photos/Corbis, p. 23; © Michael Wheatley/Alamy, p. 24; The Granger Collection, New York, pp. 25, 33 © Stock Montage/Getty Images, p. 28; © William Brooks/Alamy, p. 32; Library of Congress (LC-DIG-npcc-01259), p. 35; © Hemis/Alamy, p. 37; AP Photo/Al Grillo, p. 38; © Luis Sinco/Los Angeles Times/Getty Images, p. 39; Annik MH de Carufel/Sipa USA/Newcom, p. 40.

Front cover: © iStockphoto.com/WendyOlsenPhotography.